Nuclear Power

Examining Cause and Effect Relationships

Curriculum Consultant: JoAnne Buggey, Ph.D.
College of Education, University of Minnesota

By Neal Bernards

Greenhaven Press, Inc.
Post Office Box 289009
San Diego, CA 92198-0009

Titles in the opposing viewpoints juniors series:

AIDS	The Palestinian Conflict
Alcohol	Patriotism
Animal Rights	Poverty
Death Penalty	Prisons
Drugs and Sports	Smoking
The Environment	Television
Gun Control	Toxic Wastes
The Homeless	The U.S. Constitution
Immigration	Working Mothers
Nuclear Power	Zoos

Library of Congress Cataloging-in-Publication Data

Bernards, Neal, 1963–
    Nuclear power: examining cause and effect relationships / by Neal
Bernards.
        p.   cm. — (Opposing viewpoints juniors)
    Summary: Presents opposing viewpoints on various aspects of
nuclear power, including the questions of whether it is necessary,
safe, or desired by people in this country.
    ISBN 0-89908-607-1
    1. Nuclear energy—Juvenile literature.   [1. Nuclear energy.]
I. Title.   II. Series.
TK9148.B47 1990
333.792′4—dc20   90-40412
                                                                  CIP
                                                                  AC

Cover photo: © 1989, Martin Rogers/FPG International

CONTENTS

The Purpose of This Book: An Introduction to Opposing Viewpoints............................4
Skill Introduction: Examining Cause and Effect Relationships........................5
Sample Viewpoint A: I believe nuclear power is dangerous................................6
Sample Viewpoint B: I don't think nuclear power is very dangerous....................7
Analyzing the
Sample Viewpoints: Tallying Cause and Effect......................................8

Chapter **1**

Preface: Is Nuclear Power Necessary?..9
Viewpoint 1:   Nuclear power is necessary..................................10
Viewpoint 2:   Nuclear power is unnecessary..............................12
Critical Thinking Skill 1:   Examining Cause and Effect.............................14

Chapter **2**

Preface: Is Nuclear Power Safe?..15
Viewpoint 3:   Nuclear power is safe......................................16
Viewpoint 4:   Nuclear power is unsafe....................................18
Critical Thinking Skill 2:   Examining Cause and Effect.............................20

Chapter **3**

Preface: How Harmful Is Nuclear Waste?.................................21
Viewpoint 5:   Nuclear waste is harmful..................................22
Viewpoint 6:   Nuclear waste is not harmful............................24
Critical Thinking Skill 3:   Writing an Essay Using Cause and Effect
                          Arguments..26

Chapter **4**

Preface: Do Americans Want Nuclear Power?..........................27
Viewpoint 7:   The American public supports nuclear power.....................28
Viewpoint 8:   The American public does not support nuclear power...........30
Critical Thinking Skill 4:   Examining Cause and Effect in
                          Editorial Cartoons.................................32

An Introduction to Opposing Viewpoints

When people disagree, it is hard to figure out who is right. You may decide one person is right just because the person is your friend or a relative. But this is not a very good reason to agree or disagree with someone. It is better if you try to understand why these people disagree. On what main points do they differ? Read or listen to each person's argument carefully. Separate the facts and opinions that each person presents. Finally, decide which argument best matches what you think. This process, examining an argument without emotion, is part of what critical thinking is all about.

This is not easy. Many things make it hard to understand and form opinions. People's values, ages, and experiences all influence the way they think. This is why learning to read and think critically is an invaluable skill. Opposing Viewpoints Juniors books will help

you learn and practice skills to improve your ability to read critically. By reading opposing views on an issue, you will become familiar with methods people use to attempt to convince you that their point of view is right. And you will learn to separate the authors' opinions from the facts they present.

Each Opposing Viewpoints Juniors book focuses on one critical thinking skill that will help you judge the views presented. Some of these skills are telling fact from opinion, recognizing propaganda techniques, and locating and analyzing the main idea. These skills will allow you to examine opposing viewpoints more easily. Each viewpoint in this book is paraphrased from the original to make it easier to read. The viewpoints are placed in a running debate and are always placed with the pro view first.

Examining Cause and Effect Relationships

In this Opposing Viewpoints Juniors book, you will learn to recognize cause and effect statements, a basic critical thinking skill. By learning how to identify cause and effect, you will be able to evaluate the reasons authors give for their arguments.

In the readings in this book, the authors take different stands on the issue of nuclear power. The authors disagree on the safety of nuclear power and whether or not it should be used to supply America's future energy needs. You will be asked to identify the causes and effects each author supplies to prove his/her argument. Next, you will be asked to analyze them: For example, does the author's reasoning seem logical? Or are the cause and effect claims exaggerated or irrelevant? Finally, in the critical-thinking activities at the end of each pair of viewpoints, you will be asked to compare the evidence presented by the authors and attempt to determine which one has presented the most logical causes and effects.

We asked two students to give their opinions on the issue of nuclear power. Examine their viewpoints. Look for examples of cause and effect in their arguments.

I believe nuclear power is dangerous.

I think nuclear power is bad because it releases radiation into the air and water. I remember hearing about the Chernobyl nuclear disaster and how much harm it caused. Scientists think that the people who live within hundreds of miles of the plant might get cancer because of the radiation. People still can't live there. And cows can't eat the grass grown near the plant.

My older brother says nuclear power plants can explode just like nuclear bombs because they both use uranium. I think it's stupid to build something that dangerous.

I don't think nuclear power is very dangerous.

Nuclear power is no more dangerous than anything else we do to produce energy. Power plants that burn coal pollute the air and cause acid rain. Power plants that burn oil force us to use huge ships that sometimes spill oil. Nuclear power is safer and cleaner than coal or oil.

I think people overreact to what they read in the newspapers about radiation from nuclear power plants. It's not that bad. I heard that if you live close to a nuclear plant for a year, it's the same as having one x-ray. That doesn't seem like very much radiation.

Brian and Emily have very different opinions about the issue of using nuclear power. Both of them give examples of cause and effect in their arguments.

Brian:

CAUSE	EFFECT
Chernobyl released radiation into the atmosphere.	People can't live there. Cows can't eat the grass.

Emily:

CAUSE	EFFECT
Coal-burning plants pollute the air. Newspaper stories are written about radiation.	Acid rain. People are afraid of nuclear power.

In this sample, Brian and Emily have very different beliefs about the dangers of nuclear power. Both Brian and Emily think they are right about nuclear power. What conclusions would you come to from this sample? Whom do you agree with? Why? As you continue to read through the viewpoints in this book, try keeping a tally like the one above to compare the authors' arguments.

CHAPTER 1

PREFACE: Is Nuclear Power Necessary?

Almost 20 percent of America's electrical energy is supplied by nuclear power. In countries like France and Belgium, over half of the electricity comes from nuclear power.

Many scientists, like those who work for the Nuclear Regulatory Commission, believe the U.S. should follow France's example and depend more on nuclear power. They claim that nuclear power is necessary to guarantee a strong future for America. Without it, many people believe that the U.S. will not have enough energy to keep businesses and industries running smoothly.

Opponents of nuclear power disagree. These critics include members of Greenpeace, Earth First, Nuclear Freeze, and other environmental and anti-nuclear groups. Unlike the scientists, these people claim that nuclear power might destroy America's future. They fear a nuclear accident could release harmful radiation into the atmosphere. Opponents of nuclear power argue that safe alternatives, such as hydroelectric dams, solar power, windmills, geothermal power, and burning garbage, exist as alternatives to generating electricity.

The following viewpoints debate the issue of whether or not nuclear power is necessary. As you read, keep track of the cause and effect arguments used by the authors. Which author seems to build the strongest case?

Editor's Note: The author of this viewpoint says that nuclear power is the best source of electrical energy available. He argues that no other energy source can meet America's growing energy needs. As you read, note the cause and effect arguments used by the author.

The author claims that the U.S. need for electricity has the effect of making nuclear power necessary.

How does energy use effect the economy?

For America to grow and prosper it must have electricity—lots of electricity. The cheapest, most reliable form of this electricity is generated in nuclear power plants. No other way to produce energy can be counted on to keep pace with America's growing population and industry.

From 1949 to 1973, the U.S. enjoyed the healthiest business climate in its history. During that time, U.S. energy use also rose. Generally, when a country's economy is doing well, new businesses are started, factories are built, and stores are opened, thus requiring more energy. This relationship between energy use and a good economy proves that rising energy needs must be met to insure a healthy future. And the best way to meet those energy needs is with nuclear power. If nuclear power plants were abandoned, the American economy would suffer.

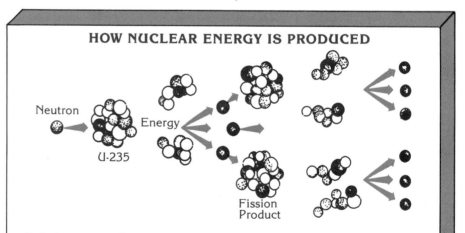

HOW NUCLEAR ENERGY IS PRODUCED

Neutron — U-235 — Energy — Fission Product

Radiation consists of tiny particles given off by atoms. Atoms are the building blocks that make up everything in the universe. The center of the atom, the nucleus, is made up of small particles called protons and neutrons.

Most atoms are stable. This means that if they are left alone, they will not break apart. But if an extra neutron is either added or taken away from an atomic nucleus, the atom becomes unstable. In order to regain its stability, the atom must get rid of something. This might be a proton, a neutron (or both), or some other kind of particle. This process is called atomic decay. The particles that are given off by the atom are radiation.

Small amounts of radiation are quite common in nature. Normal traces can be found in the rocks of the earth's crust and even in animals and human beings. This "background" radiation is not dangerous.

SOURCE: U.S. Dept. of Energy

The oil crisis of the mid-1970s taught us that the U.S. cannot rely on foreign countries for its energy supplies. When the Oil Producing and Exporting Countries (OPEC) raised the price of oil, Americans suffered because gas became more expensive. Lines at gas stations legthened due to the artificially imposed oil "shortage." Car owners could no longer drive wherever and whenever they pleased. Electricity rates also increased since the oil for oil-burning plants had become more expensive. This oil crisis proved that the American economy could be controlled by other nations.

What effect does the author say the oil crisis had on the U.S.?

With abundant nuclear power, the U.S. could cut out its need for oil to generate electricity. American dependence on foreign oil would lessen because uranium is in great supply. Former U.S. Secretary of Energy John S. Herrington writes, "Nuclear power is safe, efficient, and necessary for our nation's future energy security." Herrington says America must rely on nuclear power, not oil, for its future energy needs.

Some people think coal and oil are better sources of energy than nuclear power. They claim that coal and oil-burning plants are simple, cheap, and much safer than nuclear plants. Alan S. Manne and Richard G. Richels disagree. Manne is a professor of operations research at Stanford University, and Richels works for the Electrical Power Research Institute. They write, "If the principal alternatives to nuclear power were cheap, plentiful, reliable, and clean, the choice would be easy. But there are no easy choices." Manne and Richels say that coal, while cheap, is dirty. They argue that, in addition, coal-fired power plants contribute to acid rain. Air pollution caused by coal-burning plants may also cause higher cancer rates. As we have seen, using oil to produce energy is not a good option.

According to the author, what effect do coal-fired plants have on the environment?

Until better sources of energy become available, nuclear power remains the only proven, reliable energy source. If a switch is made to alternative forms of energy, the U.S. might experience widespread power shortages and economic ruin. For America to succeed in this century and the next, nuclear power must continue to be developed.

What does the author say would cause the U.S. to experience power shortages and economic ruin? Does his argument seem reasonable?

Nuclear power and America's needs

The author believes nuclear power is necessary to help America's economic growth. What evidence does he give? What effect does he say halting nuclear energy would have on America?

Editor's Note: The following viewpoint lists many reasons why nuclear power is unnecessary. The author writes that people can learn to conserve energy and thus reduce the need for new energy sources. Look for examples of cause and effect arguments.

America would be a better, healthier country without nuclear power. While electrical energy is necessary for the U.S., it does not have to come from nuclear power plants. Cheaper, safer forms of energy are available.

Supporters of nuclear power argue that it is cheaper than other forms of energy. That is not true. The incredibly high cost of building complex nuclear power plants raises the energy costs to consumers. The laws governing nuclear power plants are strict. This means that expensive safety devices must be built into the plants to keep lethal radiation from leaking into the environment. Cost overruns in building plants now reach into the billion-dollar range.

Another problem is how to dispose of the radioactive waste produced by nuclear power plants. Special containers, trucks, trains, and workers must be used to transport old uranium to burial sites. There, the barrels of nuclear waste are placed in

According to the author, how do tough laws affect the cost of nuclear power?

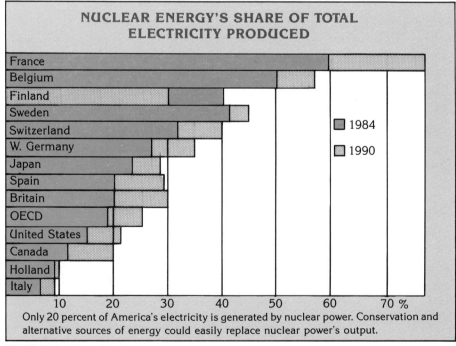

NUCLEAR ENERGY'S SHARE OF TOTAL ELECTRICITY PRODUCED

France
Belgium
Finland
Sweden
Switzerland
W. Germany
Japan
Spain
Britain
OECD
United States
Canada
Holland
Italy

1984
1990

10   20   30   40   50   60   70 %

Only 20 percent of America's electricity is generated by nuclear power. Conservation and alternative sources of energy could easily replace nuclear power's output.

SOURCE: Nuclear Energy Agency

concrete-lined pits and covered with dirt. This process is expensive and still does not solve the problem of nuclear wastes; it just buries it. Future generations may end up paying extraordinary sums to clean up the mess these barrels make. So while nuclear power may be cheaper for our generation, the true costs may be borne by our grandchildren.

Who does the author say will pay for nuclear power?

To fight the high cost of nuclear power, Americans could conserve energy. If the right measures are taken, conservation could make nuclear power unnecessary. Already conservation has succeeded on a limited scale. Since the oil crisis of the mid-1970s, Americans' energy use has leveled off. People have realized that insulating their homes, driving less, and turning off more lights did not take much effort, but it saved a lot of energy.

Physicist Amory B. Lovins and lawyer L. Hunter Lovins see even more promise for conservation in the future. They argue that equipment using advanced technology, rather than requiring more energy, would use less. They believe this is the right direction to take to satisfy increasing energy needs. Rather than building new power plants, the Lovins think Americans should stop wasting energy. They write, "Our whole economy is like someone who cannot keep the bathtub full because the water keeps running out; before we buy a bigger nuclear- or coal-powered plant, we really ought to get a plug."

The author argues that conservation could affect energy sources. What proof does he give to support this statement?

There are other good, clean forms of energy that can be used to provide America's energy needs. Jeannine Honicker has long fought the construction of nuclear power plants. She voices the thoughts of many when she writes, "We don't need nuclear pollution. We can and must produce electricity from non-nuclear, renewable sources. Harness the wind, the sun, the tides. Burn municipal garbage to cool and heat homes and offices; tap methane from existing landfills. Cogenerate electricity from industrial waste steam. Turn wood waste into charcoal, dig for geothermal power, burn alcohol." Together, these alternatives could provide safe energy to keep America strong.

What effect does Honicker say alternative forms of energy will have on the environment?

Nuclear power is not cheap. It is not safe. And it is not necessary.

The alternatives to nuclear energy

The author says the oil crisis caused Americans to evaluate their energy use. According to the author, what was the effect?

The authors of Viewpoints 1 and 2 have very different opinions on the necessity of nuclear power. They also have very different ideas on the effects of nuclear power on the environment. In answering the margin questions, you have already thought about many of the causes and effects the authors presented. In this activity, you will review some of these and compare and contrast the authors' reasoning.

Nuclear power is necessary

CAUSE	EFFECT
America's energy needs	need to build more nuclear power plants
coal-fired power plants	acid rain and higher cancer rates

Nuclear power is unnecessary

CAUSE	EFFECT
complex rules governing nuclear plants	high cost of nuclear energy
oil crisis	conservation of energy

In Viewpoint 1, the author attempts to prove that nuclear power is necessary. What evidence does the author offer that this is true? Does the author's conclusion seem logical? Why or why not?

In Viewpoint 2, the author offers proof to support a different conclusion. What evidence does the author present to prove his case that nuclear power is unnecessary? Do his conclusions seem logical? Why or why not?

Which viewpoint do you personally believe presents the best case for or against nuclear power? Why?

CHAPTER 2

PREFACE: Is Nuclear Power Safe?

For years, nuclear power supporters claimed that no one had ever died from a nuclear mishap. Then, on April 25, 1986, that changed. The Chernobyl nuclear power plant in the Ukraine exploded when the cooling water in its fuel core was accidently drained. The plant spewed a vast cloud of radiation into the atmosphere that eventually circled the earth. Twenty-six Soviets died in the weeks following the accident. Hundreds more were exposed to high levels of cancer-causing radiation. It was the worst nuclear accident in history.

Critics of nuclear power used the accident to prove that nuclear power is not worth the risk. The radiation from Chernobyl affected tens of thousands of Soviet citizens. Many were forced from their homes. Others fell ill. Hundreds of square miles of once-prosperous land now lie fallow because of radiation contamination. A larger nuclear accident than Chernobyl could kill thousands, poison the land and water for hundreds of miles, and cause a radiation cloud to drift around the earth. Opponents of nuclear power claim these dire risks make it too dangerous for widespread use.

Supporters of nuclear power, on the other hand, view the accident in a positive light. They agree that the Chernobyl accident was bad. However, they point out that less than fifty people died in this horrible mishap. To them, it proves that the public's fear is exaggerated. The worst has happened, supporters claim, and the world survived.

As you can see, the causes and effects of nuclear power are much in debate. As you read the next two viewpoints, try to analyze the differences in the authors' arguments.

Editor's Note: In the following viewpoint, the author argues that the nuclear power industry is governed by strict rules that make large accidents impossible. The author blames the media for exaggerating the risk of a nuclear accident.

According to the author, which has caused more deaths, nuclear power or coal-burning plants?

The Three Mile Island accident frightened many people. What positive effect does the author think the accident had?

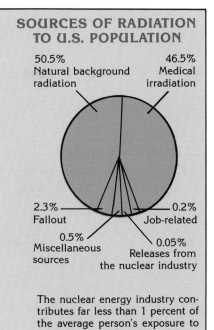

SOURCES OF RADIATION TO U.S. POPULATION

50.5% Natural background radiation

46.5% Medical irradiation

2.3% Fallout

0.2% Job-related

0.5% Miscellaneous sources

0.05% Releases from the nuclear industry

The nuclear energy industry contributes far less than 1 percent of the average person's exposure to radiation.

SOURCE: National Academy of Sciences, 1980; National Council of Radiation Protection and Measurement, 1984

Nuclear power is the safest form of energy used in the world today. While less than fifty people have died in nuclear-related accidents, thousands have died in coal-mining disasters and from breathing polluted air.

It is highly unlikely that any widespread death will occur from a nuclear power plant. The simple reason? The Nuclear Regulatory Commission requires stringent safeguards on the plants. More rules apply to nuclear power than to any other industry in the world. In the aftermath of the accident at the Three Mile Island nuclear power plant near Harrisburg, Pennsylvania, safety precautions are even more rigorous than before.

Many improvements have been made to reactors in the U.S. First, the nuclear reaction between the uranium fuel rods can be stopped at any time. In an emergency, operators can drop control rods, usually made of boron, between the uranium rods to absorb the shooting neutrons. This is called "scramming." Scramming makes the possibility of a "meltdown," or overheating of the uranium, almost impossible. Second, a back-up water-cooling system exists in case the water level in the reacting pool gets too low. And finally, a building with four-foot-thick walls, called a containment structure, is built over the reactor. This prevents radiation from escaping into the atmosphere in the unlikely event of an accident. These redundant safety measures are more than adequate to protect the public from radiation.

In reality, the greatest danger from nuclear power occurs because of the media. Over the years, newspaper and television reporters have led the public to believe a nuclear accident could destroy or pollute the entire country. Minor nuclear mishaps have gotten major coverage, while more serious accidents involving coal-mine fires and cave-ins have received scant attention. The media have caused the public to panic. For example, after the accident at Three Mile Island, media reports said that cows' milk might be contaminated by radiation for hundreds of miles around the plant. That report was false. While some slightly higher traces of radiation were found in the milk from around Three Mile Island, it was nowhere near as serious as reported. The media enjoys using these stories to feed the public's fear of radiation. Since most reporters do not understand nuclear power, they like to make it a modern-day scapegoat for environmental problems instead of reporting about deaths in coal mines or pollution from oil-burning power plants.

People will believe what the media tell them. If the media say radiation remains harmful for thousands of years, then the public thinks that every dose of radiation is potentially lethal. The media has presented a biased, unbalanced view of nuclear power.

The media could correct this problem by telling people the truth about nuclear energy. That truth is that it is the safest form of electrical power available. More people die each year from breathing polluted air from coal-fired plants than have died in the entire history of nuclear power. As prize-winning nuclear physicist Bernard L. Cohen argues, "An average nuclear meltdown is estimated to cause four hundred deaths, which means that for nuclear energy to match the ten thousand deaths per year from coal burning, there would have to be a meltdown every two weeks."

Nuclear physicist Anthony V. Nero, Jr., certainly understands the risks and dangers of nuclear energy. However, Nero writes that "nuclear power must be considered one of our principal energy options for the foreseeable future. It is, indeed, safe enough."

The author says that nuclear power is not dangerous. But what effect does the media have on people's attitude about nuclear power?

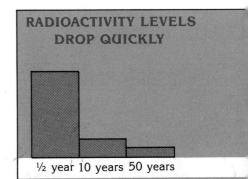

RADIOACTIVITY LEVELS DROP QUICKLY

½ year 10 years 50 years

In a nuclear power plant, the level of radioactivity falls rapidly during the time just after plant shut-down. The figure illustrates this decrease in radioactivity (contamination and induced radioactivity) in a 1000 MWe light-water reactor after shutdown.

SOURCE: The American Nuclear Society

What effect does Cohen say a nuclear accident would have? Why does he say that this is not very bad?

A safe form of energy

The author says that the Three Mile Island accident caused some things to change in the nuclear power industry. Name them. The author also claims that the public's fear of nuclear accidents is exaggerated and affects the development of nuclear power. How?

Editor's Note: The author of the following viewpoint writes that the accident at Chernobyl caused the world to understand the dangers of nuclear power. The author claims that the ever-present possibility of an accident makes using nuclear power too risky.

According to the author, what caused illnesses in the Soviet Union?

What effect did the accident at Chernobyl have, in the author's opinion?

It is foolish to claim that nuclear power is safe. Anyone who viewed the photos of the devastated nuclear power plant at Chernobyl knows better. Nuclear power cannot be used without grave damage to our environment. Even years after the world's worst nuclear accident, the radiation levels at Chernobyl are dangerously high. And thousands of Soviets are still suffering from radiation-caused illnesses such as leukemia and thyroid cancer.

No matter how much electricity nuclear power may provide, Chernobyl proves that it is too unsafe for common use. The world cannot afford higher rates of cancer and radiation-contaminated food in areas around nuclear power plants. Numerous studies have been done about the effects of a nuclear accident. Almost all of these studies reveal that thousands of people would die. Even reports by the Nuclear Regulatory Commission (NRC), which normally promotes nuclear power, are extremely frightening.

A 1975 report to the NRC claimed that a "worst case" accident would mean 3,300 immediate deaths. In addition, the report predicted 45,000 eventual deaths from cancer, 45,000 victims

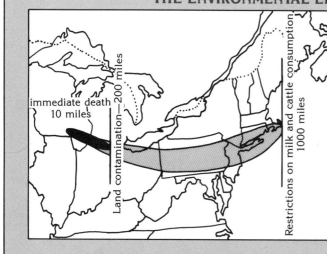

THE ENVIRONMENTAL EFFECTS OF A MELTDOWN

immediate death 10 miles

Land contamination—200 miles

Restrictions on milk and cattle consumption 1000 miles

Fission products traveling downwind in a rough 10° angle from an uncontrolled meltdown at a nuclear power plant in Wisconsin would have widespread effects on the area in their path. Our computer studies show that there will be immediate fatalities within 10 miles of the reactor, land contamination out to 200 miles, and restrictions on milk and cattle consumption out to 1000 miles. There would also be latent cancer deaths up to 1000 miles from the reactor.

SOURCE: Redrawn from NUCLEAR POWER: BOTH SIDES, The Best Arguments for and Against the Most Controversial Technology, Edited by Michio Kaku, Ph.D., and Jennifer Trainer, by permission of W. W. Norton & Company, Inc. Copyright © 1982 by Michio Kaku and Jennifer Trainer.

requiring hospital treatment, 240,000 people suffering from thyroid tumors, and 5,000 children born with genetic defects. No argument for nuclear power can counter such disturbing numbers.

Time and again we are told that layers of safety measures protect the public from accidents at nuclear power plants. But if nuclear power is so safe, why are the newspapers filled with stories about accidents? Why is the area around Chernobyl now a wasteland? And if these new plants keep breaking down, what will happen when they get old?

Nuclear power plants like Chernobyl and Three Mile Island are supposed to generate electricity for twenty to thirty years. Neither of these two lasted nearly that long. If a deadly accident like the one at the ultra-modern Chernobyl plant can occur, what might happen thirty years from now when pipes, valves, and electronic equipment begin to wear out? Russell Peterson, who served on a commission that studied the Three Mile Island accident, says that the chance of failure increases as a nuclear power plant ages.

Some people believe that even these alarming predictions of deadly nuclear accidents are too conservative. Jan Beyea, a staff physicist for the National Audubon Society, compares the nuclear industry of today to the auto industry of 1905. Back then, cars were a new item. They were also slow and few in number. No one could foresee the impact they would have on American society—especially that fifty thousand people a year would die in auto accidents. Likewise, Beyea says, no one can truly predict what will happen with nuclear power because it is still so new. Over time, Americans may come to regret relying on this dangerous technology.

The poor history of nuclear power should cause all Americans to call for a stop in building more plants. The ones operating now should be taken out of service as soon as possible. The risk of radiation contamination is too great. Nuclear power is not safe, and it will never be safe. Ask any Soviet who used to live in Chernobyl.

How would a nuclear accident affect thousands of people? What proof does the author offer?

What does the author think will happen when nuclear power plants get old?

The author compares the effect cars have had on human health to the effect of nuclear power. Does this seem like a good comparison? Why or why not?

Nuclear power and deadly accidents

Why does the author believe nuclear power is unsafe? What effect does he say a major nuclear accident would have?

After reading this viewpoint and the previous viewpoint, do you agree with this author that nuclear power is unsafe? Why or why not?

Examining Cause and Effect

This activity will allow you to practice examining cause and effect relationships. The statements below focus on the subject matter of this book. Read each paragraph and consider it carefully. For each paragraph, identify the cause and effect relationship.

If you are doing this activity as a member of a class or group, compare your answers with other class or group members. You will find that others may have different answers than you do. Listening to the reasons others give for their answers can help you in examining cause and effect.

EXAMPLE: Nuclear power plants release small amounts of radiation into the atmosphere. People living near nuclear plants have a higher rate of cancer, thyroid problems, and birth defects.

Cause: radiation   **Effect:** cancer, thyroid problems, and birth defects

1. Milk taken from cows near the Three Mile Island nuclear power plant contained cancer-causing radiation.

   Cause _____ Effect _____

2. People are too afraid of nuclear power plants. They forget that without the electricity from nuclear power plants they would have to pay a higher price for their electricity.

   Cause _____ Effect _____

3. People want to protect the atmosphere from radiation, but they don't understand that coal-burning power plants pollute the air with sulfur and other chemicals. A little radiation is better than a lot of air pollutants.

   Cause _____ Effect _____

4. Our world is delicate and perfectly balanced. One or two bad nuclear accidents could permanently pollute the air, land, and water. We must protect our natural environment from radiation.

   Cause _____ Effect _____

PREFACE: How Harmful Is Nuclear Waste?

Nuclear power plants generate large amounts of nuclear waste that must be disposed of properly to protect the public from harm. At present, most waste is stored in temporary holding pools located within the plants themselves. However, these pools are quickly filling up, and new storage spaces must be found. Nuclear waste not stored in pools is packed in barrels, shipped to toxic waste dumps, and buried. But some barrels have started to leak, and public officials worry that the groundwater near these dumps has become polluted. No permanent solution yet exists for the problem of what to do with nuclear waste.

What is radioactive nuclear waste? It includes the uranium fuel rods, their cooling water, the walls surrounding the reactor, and tailings left over from mined uranium. Anything that is exposed to radiation during the nuclear reaction must be disposed of properly. This waste remains at dangerous radioactive levels for hundreds of years.

Critics of nuclear power claim that nuclear waste can never be stored safely. They say that if buried underground, radioactive waste can leak out and pollute the water supply. If dumped in the ocean, it can kill sea animals. And if left in temporary storage, it can leak out or be accidently dug up.

Supporters of nuclear power point out that nuclear waste has not been a problem. They argue that the public has never suffered any illnesses from nuclear waste and that plans are being made to find permanent solutions.

The viewpoints in this chapter debate whether nuclear waste can ever be safely managed. Watch for the cause and effect arguments used by the authors to support their arguments.

This viewpoint lists the reasons that nuclear waste poses environmental problems. In it, the author writes that current storage methods have released radiation into the earth's atmosphere. The author uses numerous cause and effect arguments to support his case.

According to the author, what will happen if nuclear waste keeps piling up?

Nuclear waste is piling up in America at alarming rates. This waste is an accident waiting to happen. Either nuclear waste will be spilled during shipment, or it will leak out during storage. It is a no-win situation. The nuclear industry's poor management of this waste proves that it is highly dangerous and that they do not know how to store it safely.

Why does the author think the public has lost faith in the government's ability to handle nuclear waste?

There has never been a plan for what to do with nuclear waste. Leaders in the Atomic Energy Commission and, later, in the Department of Energy were so excited about their new technology that they never considered its safety. James J. MacKenzie, the senior staff scientist for the Union of Concerned Scientists, writes that "tanks holding high-level wastes have leaked unnoticed, as have dumps where low-level wastes were buried." From this, MacKenzie rightly thinks that the public no longer believes the U.S. government can handle the problem. For years they neglected to find a solution, and soon it may be too late.

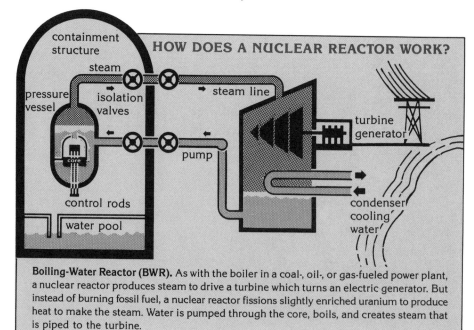

HOW DOES A NUCLEAR REACTOR WORK?

containment structure

steam

pressure vessel

isolation valves

steam line

turbine generator

pump

core

control rods

water pool

condenser cooling water

Boiling-Water Reactor (BWR). As with the boiler in a coal-, oil-, or gas-fueled power plant, a nuclear reactor produces steam to drive a turbine which turns an electric generator. But instead of burning fossil fuel, a nuclear reactor fissions slightly enriched uranium to produce heat to make the steam. Water is pumped through the core, boils, and creates steam that is piped to the turbine.

SOURCE: Atomic Industrial Forum, Inc.

Unfortunately, the problem cannot be ignored. It will not simply go away. In her report, *Decommissioning Nuclear Plants*, Cynthia Pollock writes, "Nuclear plants cannot simply be abandoned at the end of their operating lives or demolished with a wrecking ball. Radioactivity builds up each year the plant operates, and all the contaminated parts and equipment must be securely isolated from people and the environment." Dismantling and removing this much radioactive material from each nuclear power plant is time-consuming and expensive.

What causes waste storage to be so expensive, according to Pollock?

Money would not be an issue if the public could be guaranteed safety, but they cannot. Waste stored deep in mines will heat up over time. The surrounding rock will in turn be heated, causing it to expand. Once it expands, it may crack and allow water to seep into the storage area. The contaminated water might then flow into drinking water or otherwise return to the earth's surface. No method of disposal, however clever, can ever be foolproof. While underground storage might work for a couple of hundred years, the radiation from nuclear waste can last a thousand. Exposing our great-grandchildren to cancer-causing radiation is not an acceptable solution.

The author claims that underground storage is not a perfect solution. What effect does he think it would have?

Some people have suggested shooting radioactive waste into deep space. The explosion of the shuttle *Challenger* should quiet all supporters of that theory. Dumping waste in the sea is also not an acceptable solution since tides, underwater currents, and temperature differences could cause the radiation to drift away from its dump site. And since the ocean covers 75 percent of the earth's surface, it would be foolish to pollute it.

The highly dangerous nature of nuclear waste makes it impossible to manage. Though some method must be found to store the waste that now exists, there is no reason to create more. Nuclear power involves more than keeping the plant safe; it involves dealing with waste for hundreds of years to come. It is not worth the effort.

Why does the author say radioactive waste is impossible to manage?

Can nuclear waste be stored?

The author believes that storing nuclear waste in mines might have some harmful effects. Name them. Why does the author argue that waste should not be dumped into the ocean or blasted into space? Do you agree with this argument? Why or why not?

Editor's Note: In this viewpoint, the author argues that radioactive waste is not as big a problem as Americans are led to believe. The author writes that television and newspapers have created an irrational fear of radiation. Note the author's use of cause and effect arguments.

Does the author offer proof that radioactive waste is not harmful?

In the author's view, what effects would burying waste underground prevent?

Like any technical problem, the issue of nuclear waste will be solved over time. Presently, the American public is in no danger from nuclear waste, nor will it ever be. The holding pools and storage tanks at the nuclear power plants that now house the waste are perfectly safe. Equally safe are the specially built dump sites where low-level radioactive waste is buried beneath layers of protective soil.

More permanent plans call for the waste to be buried deep within the earth. One proposed solution is to store the waste in old mines, two thousand feet or more beneath the earth's surface. The mines that would be used were dug into very stable rock that would keep the waste protected for hundreds of years. No radiation would seep into the groundwater. No earthquakes or eruptions would bring radiation to the surface. And since the original mine entrance will be plugged, no radiation would ever be able to escape into the air.

Reprinted by permission of 21st Century Science Associates, PO Box 17285, Washington, D.C., 20041.

Some nuclear scientists propose that another safeguard be added to these underground storage sites. They think the waste should first be encased in glass blocks and then sealed in stainless-steel containers. These materials would prevent rust. Normally, nuclear waste tends to heat up over time, especially if stored compactly. One design, therefore, calls for the containers to be at least thirty feet apart in order to prevent heat build-up and possible rupturing of the containers.

These safeguards for storing radioactive waste should calm the fears of the public. Nuclear physicist Bernard L. Cohen writes, "Even if *all* of the radioactivity in nuclear waste burial grounds were to leak out and spread through the soil, there would probably never be a single death." Cohen explains that the radiation would only have one chance in a billion of getting into human food and one chance in 100,000 of entering a person's lungs. These slight risks shouldn't stop nuclear power.

What effect does Cohen say a radiation leak would have?

The most difficult part of storing nuclear waste is finding people who will allow the waste to be buried in their state. Residents of Nevada have fought to keep nuclear waste out of old mines in their barren state. Hysterical headlines in Nevada newspapers lead people to believe that they would automatically get cancer if they lived near a waste disposal area. These irrational fears are fanned by reports that birth defects or cancer rates are higher than normal in areas near nuclear power plants and waste storage sites.

In the author's opinion, who has caused the most problems with storing waste?

The trouble with these reports is that they do not examine other possible causes for those cancer rates and birth defects. For example, the people in the area may smoke more or drink more than the average population. Or the air may be polluted, or the water they drink may be tainted. A disease is often caused by several factors, not just one, as the reports would lead people to believe.

Why does the author question the link between waste storage sites and cancer rates? What other causes does he suggest might account for the reports' findings?

As John Herrington, the former U.S. Secretary of Energy, says, "We have a nuclear waste act, and we have a nuclear waste plan." Now if people would stop blocking the progress that is being made in solving the nuclear waste problem, it could be taken care of easily.

Should nuclear waste be stored in underground mines?

Why does the author believe that storing radioactive waste in old mines will work? Knowing what you do about radiation, does the author make a good case for storing waste in mines? Why or why not?

CRITICAL THINKING SKILL 3

Writing an Essay Using Cause and Effect Arguments

In this book we have been studying cause and effect arguments. Authors writing about environmental and health-related issues often use this type of argument to support their cases. This activity will allow you to practice your skill in using cause and effect arguments to write an essay.

Read the cartoon below. What cause and effect argument does the cartoonist use to make his point? Which source of power does the cartoonist think is most harmful?

"FORGET NUCLEAR, YOU SAID! WE'LL SWITCH TO COAL, YOU SAID! THERE'S NO WASTE PROBLEM, YOU SAID...!"

John Trever/Albuquerque Journal. Reprinted with permission.

A. After having read the six previous viewpoints, use your knowledge to write an essay using cause and effect arguments. Choose one of the two topics listed below.

   1. Write a short essay describing why nuclear power is a better way of generating electricity than coal-burning plants. Use at least two cause and effect arguments in your essay.
   2. Write a short essay describing why coal-burning plants are a better way of generating electricity than nuclear power. Again, use at least two cause and effect arguments.

B. Compare your essays with other members of the class. Write down the cause and effect arguments the other students used in the essays you read and answer the following questions:

   1. Were the students' cause and effect arguments effective? Be prepared to explain your answer.
   2. Did the students use the same arguments you used? Are some cause and effect arguments more logical than others? Give examples.

4

PREFACE: Do Americans Want Nuclear Power?

The use of nuclear power to supply America's electricity is controversial. With the environmental movement of the late 60s and early 70s, the American public began to question the need for nuclear power.

Concerns about possible nuclear accidents near large cities have delayed the opening of plants like the one in Seabrook, New Hampshire. According to consumer advocate Ralph Nader, 15 nuclear power plants were cancelled and 122 delayed in the year after the accident at Three Mile Island. The cancellations prove that Americans are concerned about the safety of nuclear power.

Critics of nuclear power applaud the cancellations and delays in new plant construction. They argue that the American public simply does not want or need this dangerous source of energy.

On the other hand, supporters of nuclear power claim that only a small percentage of very vocal people are blocking the construction of plants that most Americans want. They claim that the well-publicized demonstrations and marches lead people to believe that most Americans are against nuclear power when that is not true. Nuclear power supporters claim the silent majority want more plants built.

As you read the viewpoints, pay attention to why the authors believe Americans support or do not support nuclear power. There are no margin questions in these two viewpoints. You must keep track of the causes and effects yourself. The focus boxes at the end of each viewpoint will ask you about the authors' arguments.

Editor's Note: The author of the following viewpoint argues that the majority of Americans support nuclear power. It is the minority of vocal protesters, he writes, who needlessly delay nuclear power plant construction. Watch for the author's use of cause and effect arguments and then answer the questions in the focus box.

Most educated Americans support the use of nuclear power to supply the nation's energy needs. These people have read articles describing the extensive safety systems used at nuclear power plants. These supporters understand that a nuclear power plant could never explode like a bomb. They know that the health risks from nuclear power are few.

Supporters of nuclear power also know that relying on nuclear power helps the country. Using nuclear power means the U.S. does not have to rely on coal or on foreign oil for its energy. With nuclear power, the U.S. is able to burn less coal and to distance itself from the Organization of Petroleum Exporting Countries (OPEC). As an editor from *The Economist* writes, "The world has good reasons for going nuclear. Countries wanted to reduce their dependence on dirty, dangerous-to-mine coal and later their dependence on OPEC oil." Using nuclear power means the U.S. can be more self-sufficient and less worried about events in the Middle East.

Americans love the latest electronic equipment and modern household appliances. These items require electricity. By using more new electronic devices, Americans consume more electricity. That electricity has to come from somewhere. Americans do not want acid rain from coal-fired plants. And they do not want to import more oil from OPEC. The only usable alternative is nuclear power. If Americans truly did not want nuclear power, they would cut back on their use of electricity. They are not cutting back. So by plugging in the VCR or using a microwave, Americans are saying they want nuclear power.

If critics of nuclear power only understood the damage coal-fired power plants cause to the environment, they would not fight nuclear power. The devastation from acid rain caused by coal-fired plants is far more harmful than the harm done by radiation.

NUCLEAR POWER IN THE UNITED STATES

● Licensed to Operate by NRC (108)
△ Under Construction (15)
✳ Planned (2)

SOURCE: U.S. Dept. of Energy

Those who demonstrate against nuclear power because they believe it harms the environment actually damage it. In blocking the use of nuclear power, demonstrators have forced the U.S. to use coal-fired power plants that belch pollution into the sky.

Part of the misunderstanding over nuclear power can be linked to the media. A five-year study showed that there were twice as many stories in the *New York Times* about radiation than there were about traffic accidents. Traffic accidents kill over fifty thousand people a year, yet radiation has killed only those who died at Chernobyl. This slanted reporting about the dangers of radiation causes unnecessary fears about nuclear power. With education, people will support nuclear power as the best answer to America's energy needs. According to Lynn R. Wallis, a consultant for General Electric on nuclear energy, 69 percent of Americans believe nuclear power is the best energy option for the future. This majority goes quietly about their business while the demonstrators create problems. It is time for the U.S. government and the nuclear industry to realize that the American public is solidly behind nuclear power.

Do Americans support nuclear power?

According to the author, what harmful effects do protesters have on the environment? What effect does he say newspapers have on the public? List three of the author's cause and effect arguments. Do you agree with the author's conclusions? Why or why not?

In the following viewpoint, the author states that nuclear power has been forced upon American consumers. The author writes that public opinion against nuclear power will eventually shut it down. As in the previous viewpoint, carefully note the cause and effect arguments and answer the questions in the focus box at the end of this viewpoint.

The majority of Americans have never supported nuclear power. From the beginning, nuclear power has been forced on U.S. consumers by the government and by big business. Only after the accidents at Three Mile Island and Chernobyl did most people fully understand its dangers.

Environment magazine said that in 1987, 49 percent of Americans were against building more nuclear power plants. Only 46 percent supported the use of nuclear power, and 6 percent were undecided. This poll was taken one year after the accident at Chernobyl. The horrible effects of Chernobyl changed the minds of many Americans who used to support nuclear power.

Aside from the accidents at Chernobyl and Three Mile Island, even more Americans have turned away from nuclear power because of the nuclear waste problem. Taxpayers are unwilling to pay the incredibly high cost of taking apart old reactors and storing the radioactive waste. They realize now that the nuclear industry lied to them about the cheap cost of nuclear power. While they cannot do anything about the plants already built,

Dan Wasserman/The Boston Globe. © 1988, Los Angeles Times Syndicate. Reprinted with permission.

protesters can block the construction of new ones. For years, construction on the Diablo Canyon nuclear power plant in California was blocked because it was being built on an earthquake fault line. The operation of the Seabrook plant in New Hampshire continues to be delayed fifteen years after its construction began. These incidents prove that Americans do not want more plants creating nuclear waste.

More significantly, Americans do not want dangerous waste to be buried in their states. Nevada voters have rejected plans to bury waste deep in old mines out in the desert. In 1976, voters in three Michigan counties voted eight-to-one against allowing nuclear waste disposal sites to be built in their area. Americans are rising up against the nuclear industry to let their opinions be known: they do not want nuclear power plants.

Nuclear power's supporters point out that America's demand for electricity makes nuclear power necessary. That is not true. Traditionally, Americans demanded more electricity every year simply because oil and coal were cheap. But oil is no longer cheap, and coal causes grave damage to the environment. Americans now know that conserving energy is a much better solution than building nuclear plants. Cars, machines, and appliances have become more energy efficient. They need less electricity now than they did twenty years ago. And more improvements can be made. Since the oil crisis, America's energy use has risen very little. The public proved to electricity producers that they would rather cut back on their electrical use than be forced to build new, dangerous nuclear power plants.

Americans are learning that they cannot pollute the earth and expect it to remain livable. One way they know to keep it clean is to prevent any new nuclear power plants from being built. Americans want their electricity to come from solar power, windmills, the tides, and geothermal steam, not from uranium. Public opinion will not allow dangerous nuclear power plants to dot the countryside.

Is nuclear power the answer?

In the author's opinion, what caused Americans to turn away from nuclear power? What effect does the author say the antinuclear movement has had on the country? After reading the two viewpoints, which do you think is more logical? Why?

4

Examining Cause and Effect in Editorial Cartoons

Throughout this book, you have seen cartoons that illustrate the ideas in the viewpoints. Editorial cartoons are an effective and usually humorous way of presenting an opinion on an issue. Cartoonists, like writers, can illustrate the concept of cause and effect in their cartoons.

The cartoon below requires some thought to understand the point it is making about nuclear power and the public. Look at the cartoon. Who does the cartoon think is responsible for poor health? What is the attitude of the man who is speaking? How does the illustration in the window further show the cartoonist's opinion of who is behind poor public health?

"First we have to convince the people that good health isn't everything."

Do you agree with the cartoonist's point in the editorial cartoon? Why or why not?

For further practice on your own, try looking at the daily newspaper for editorial cartoons. Do some of them use the concept of cause and effect to make their points?